ALL THE WORDS I SHOULD HAVE SAID

Rania Naim

AMARYLLIS

AMARYLLIS
An imprint of Manjul Publishing House Pvt. Ltd.
• C-16, Sector 3, Noida, Uttar Pradesh 201301, India
Website: www.manjulindia.com
Registered Office:
• 2nd Floor, Usha Preet Complex,
42, Malviya Nagar, Bhopal 462 003 - India
Distribution Centres
Ahmedabad, Bengaluru, Chennai, Hyderabad,
Kochi, Kolkata, Mumbai, Noida, Pune

All The Words I Should Have Said by Rania Naim

This edition first published in India in 2025

ISBN 978-93-5543-655-9

Printed and bound in India by Replika Press Private Limited

DEDICATION

To my best friend and soul sister Farah, to my mother Faten, my brother Tamer, and my aunt Hoda.

Thank you for being in my life. I wouldn't be who I am and where I am today without your love, your kindness, your support, and your guidance. I only want to make you proud.

To my lovely best friends: Thank you for believing in me and my writing and for always encouraging me to take a leap of faith. You mean the world to me, and I'll always be grateful for having you in my life.

TO MY FANS

Your words, your support, your kindness, and your stories continue to inspire me and make me want to be a better writer and a better person. This book is for you. You are the ones who keep me going and give meaning to my work. I hope I continue to write things you love and things you can relate to. Thank you. I love you.

SOMEDAY

Someday, you will look for someone
who resembles me
and on that same day
I will be with someone
who doesn't resemble you at all

THEY ASK

They ask me about my dream job
I say 'writer'
they ask me where I want to live
I say by the beach
they ask me about the universe
I tell them about the moon and the stars
then they ask me about *you*
and I never know what to say

LISTEN BUT DON'T BELIEVE

Out of courtesy
listen to all he has to say
and out of caution
believe none of it
until he proves it

INTOXICATED

You say you love me
with your shot of whiskey
you say I'm the one
with your glass of champagne
but then you don't say a word
with your cup of coffee

THERAPY

I went to a therapist
and I told him about you
he told me there's no cure
for a heart that so stubbornly clings
to what *destroys* it

I WISH I WAS YOU

I wish I loved myself more than anyone else
I wish I didn't feel bad after ignoring your text
I wish I didn't think of you every night
I wish I knew how to sleep after knowing I hurt someone
I wish I knew how to be heartless
I wish nothing fazed me
I wish I had the talent to do everything that pushes people away
yet they always want to stay
I wish I knew how to talk my way out of things
and make people believe my lies
I wish I knew how to break your heart
and call it *love*

MAKTUB

I wish I could rewrite our fate
so we can end up together
I wish I could write you for me
and write me for you
and I wish I could erase
anyone else
who came in between

TIMING

Maybe we meet the right people at the wrong time
because we wasted the *right* time with the *wrong* people

BETTER THAN ME

Everyone says
you're better than me
but I don't care
because I know that
I'm the *best* for you

WHAT YOU DESERVE

You don't deserve someone who comes back
you deserve someone who never leaves

BURNT

You tell me that I never ask about you
and I hope you know
that I'm still burnt
by the times I've asked about you
and got no response

LOVE HIM

Love him the way a woman loves
and forget him the way a man forgets

BETWEEN THE LINES

I'm afraid to text you
I'm afraid of not getting a response
I'm afraid you'd read between the lines
and know that 'hello'
means I miss you
and how have you been
means I hope I'm still on your mind
and hope you're well
means I still *love* you

YOU'RE ALLOWED TO LEAVE

You're allowed to leave any story you don't find yourself in. You're allowed to leave any story you don't love yourself in.

You're allowed to leave a city that has dimmed your light instead of making you shine brighter, you're allowed to pack all your bags and start over somewhere else, and you're allowed to redefine the *meaning* of your life.

You're allowed to quit the job you hate even if the world tells you not to and you're allowed to search for something that makes you look forward to tomorrow and to the rest of your life.

You're allowed to leave someone you love if they're treating you poorly, you're allowed to put yourself first if you're settling, and you're allowed to walk away when you've tried over and over again but nothing has changed.

You're allowed to let toxic friends go, you're allowed to surround yourself with love and people who encourage and nurture you. You're allowed to pick the kind of *energy* you need in your life.

You're allowed to forgive yourself for your biggest and smallest mistakes, and you're allowed to be kind to yourself. You're allowed to look in the mirror and actually *like* the person you see.

You're allowed to set yourself free from your own expectations.

We sometimes look at leaving as a bad thing or associate it with giving up or quitting, but sometimes leaving is the best thing you can do for yourself.

Leaving allows you to change directions, to start over, to rediscover yourself and the world. Leaving sometimes saves you from staying stuck in the wrong place with the wrong people.

Leaving opens a new door for change, growth, opportunities, and *redemption.*

You always have the choice to leave until you find where you belong and what makes you happy.

You're even allowed to leave the old you behind and reinvent yourself.

LIKE MOTHER, LIKE DAUGHTER

I asked my mom why she stayed
when she should've left
I asked her why she gave her all
and received nothing
she told me she did this for us
for her kids, for the family
then I met you
and I finally knew why she stayed
she was a woman madly in love with someone
who didn't love her back

JUST FRIENDS

I have enough friends
I don't want your friendship
I want your hand to hold at night
I want your voice to hear every morning
I want your hugs to keep me warm
I don't want your friendship
I want more
I want your love

YOU'RE JUST A BOY

You're a boy for not being honest about your intentions

You're a boy for making someone tear down their walls
only to build yours higher

You're a boy for making someone open up to you only
to close yourself off

You're a boy for promising love to someone only to
break their heart

DON'T WONDER

Don't wonder why they left
let them wonder why you never asked
Don't wonder why they stopped caring
let them wonder why you never cared to know

SUNRISES WITH YOU

I've never been a morning person
I've never been the one to wake up
when the world is sleeping
but lately I've been waking up
to watch the sunrise
and watch you sleep

TIME

I want to waste my time with you.
I want every moment to be filled with *something* of you
I want time to fly with you
or maybe I want time to *stop* with you

THE END OF THE WORLD

The city turns into a whole world
when I'm with you
since you came into my life
you became my world
and for once
I don't want the world to end

DISTANCE

Those who are distant
are those who chose to be
somewhere you're not
Those who are distant
are those who chose to live
without you

ONE-WAY STREET

She leaves without looking back
because she waited long enough
for you to look ahead

OXYMORON

Be a stranger to me
because lovers always leave

MIXED SIGNALS

I stopped decoding mixed messages
or reading between the lines
because people who care about you enough
will send you messages
you don't need to analyze or question

SOMETHING BETTER

If you're always looking for something better

you may not realize that what you have is already the best

UNCALCULATED

Don't be the one who loves more
be the one who loves without keeping score

THE CARDINAL RULE

As long as you change your pain to art
you'll never be *broken*

THE IN-BETWEEN

I'm not going to be your in-between girl
I'm either the one you always remember
or the one you wish you could forget

WAITING

Don't wait for someone to make up their mind about you
wait for someone who doesn't keep you waiting
wait for someone who wouldn't even think twice
when given the choice to be with someone like *you*

GAME OVER

Date someone who doesn't make you feel like dating them is a race you need to win

date someone who thinks you're overqualified to even participate in these ridiculous games

date someone who doesn't even want to play because the game *ended* the moment they met you

THE HANDS OF GOD

There is something liberating about handing the pen to God and letting him do his work

hand the pen to the one who doesn't need an eraser

hand the pen to the one who doesn't need help with words

hand the pen to the one who knows you better than you know yourself

hand the pen to the only one who is capable of writing your happy ending

DEATH

Death used to scare me
but now I don't know what is more terrifying
living or dying?

ONCE UPON A TIME

Once upon a time
you said you cared
Once upon a time
you wouldn't sleep without hearing my voice
Once upon a time
you said I was your everything
Once upon a time
you said you'd never let me go
and here we are
worlds apart
barely talking to each other
separated by distance and
unfulfilled promises
living in shades of what could've been
living in flashbacks of our memories
because once upon a time
you said you loved me

UNSCRIPTED

How do we know what's real?
when even the reality shows are scripted
How do we know what's real?
when even the most genuine people fool us

MY KNIGHT

I wanted you to be my knight
but you only wanted me for one night

THE ONE THAT GOT AWAY

I keep trying to find you
in everyone else
but maybe I'm not meant to find another you
because you will eventually come back to me

KEEP SCARING THEM

Maybe you scare them because you don't need them
because they know you can survive without them
because they know that you won't wait for them
because they know you will stand up for yourself
and because they know that you will not allow yourself to be
another random number on their list

But keep scaring them
keep scaring them with your honesty
with your strength
with your kindness
with your love
with your words
with your eyes
with your presence
and with your ability to read them
keep reading them until you find someone
who won't get scared off easily
someone who is just as scary as you are
so that it starts to scare *you*

STRANGERS

Here we are once more
in the same place we said we'd never be
pretending that we don't care
pretending that we never were
pretending that you didn't kiss my scars
and I didn't heal your wounds
pretending that we're both living
when we're both dying
Here we are once more
lovers then
strangers now

HER

Hold her hand tightly because secretly she doesn't want to let go

lead the way sometimes because she can get lost in her own head

speak on her behalf because her words can get lost in translation

and don't believe her when she tells you she is *fine*

because she can be carrying the weight of the world on her shoulders

but she will tell you that it's as light as a feather

DEAR GOD

Dear God,
They say that you give burdens
to those you love
but sometimes I feel
that you must love me too much

Dear God,
They say that you want me to be patient
but sometimes I wonder
how long do I have to wait
for a miracle to save me?

Dear God,
They say you always remember
the ones who pray to you
but lately I've been feeling
that maybe you've forgotten
about my prayers and about *me*

Dear God,
They say you're always listening
but sometimes I feel like you can't hear me
they say you're in every corner
but sometimes I can't find you

Dear God,
If you wanted me to make art
out of my pain
I've already created a masterpiece
when are you going to buy it?

WHAT I KNOW

I know that I'll always forgive you
no matter how many times you hurt me
I know that I'll always remember the good in you
and the way you made me feel
I know that you'll be the person who crosses my mind
when someone talks about love
I know that you'll be the one I remember
when they talk about lost love
I know that when I smile for no reason
it's because of you
and when I cry for no reason
it's also because of you
and I know that I'll still write for you
and you'll still be *out of reach*

I'M SORRY

I'm sorry you weren't able to change me
I'm sorry you had to watch someone fall out of love with you
I'm sorry you didn't succeed
in making me another one of your victims

REMEMBER ME

I want you to remember me and smile

I want you to remember me and feel like it wasn't one of those sad endings

I want you to remember that even the ending was sweet

that the ending was inevitable but it was worth it

I want you to remember that for the first time

you don't have to force yourself to forget someone

you don't have to forget about your feelings or your memories

that my name doesn't hurt when you hear it

that my pictures don't make you cringe when you see them

I want you to remember me as the first person

that proved to you that lost love is not completely lost

that we sometimes meet wonderful people who are not meant to stay forever

and that some people will always hold a special place in our hearts

because we want to *keep* them there

THE NIGHT

I only cry at night
because I get to be alone with my thoughts
I only cry at night
because that's when I remember you

I KNOW YOU'RE TIRED

You're tired of pretending you're okay

you're tired of saying there is nothing wrong with you when there is

you're tired of having to lie to people about what's going on

and you're tired of pretending to be strong and smiling

when all you want to do is cry

you wish you could just let everyone know what's wrong with you

so they can leave you alone

but you know that's not possible

and you're tired of living another day

pretending that you're not tired at all

LOSING YOU

Losing you was hard, but keeping you was harder
losing you was a lesson but not a loss
losing you was my favorite *win*

THE LOOK

You looked at her and I snapped
you said I was crazy
I said I was in love
but then you said I'm sorry
and I said I'm sorry too
but I left you that night
not because of the way you looked at her
but because of the way you *saw me*

MY FAVORITE CHAPTER

If this is the end of our story

then I want you to know that you are my favorite chapter

the chapter I will go back and read when I want to smile

the chapter I will go back and read when the story
gets boring

and I hope I'm your favorite chapter too

THE HARDEST FALL

It's like you were the fall I never really recovered from
you took the biggest part of my heart
and I'm not sure if I'll ever get it back
or if I'll be able to love again
with only half a heart

MILLION-DOLLAR QUESTIONS

Who do you run to when you're the one everyone runs to?
Who do you run to when the one you really want to run to
is running away from you?
Who do you run to when you want to run away
from yourself?

WHAT'S INSIDE

Sometimes things end and die
but they still live inside us
eating us alive

NO EXCUSES

How could I not hold it against you?
when you're alive and breathing
and still not asking about me
How could I not hold it against you?
when you're choosing not to choose me?

YOUR SECRET LANGUAGE

You speak in a language I don't understand
but I'm willing to stay up all night
studying it letter by letter
until I master every word

THE IRONY OF LIFE

It will always be this way
we love those who forget us
forget those who love us
and wonder why it never works out

PROMISE ME THIS

Promise me that you'll stay
when it's easier to leave
Promise me that you'll listen to me
when all you can hear is silence
Promise me that you'll love me
when I can't even love myself
Promise that you'll keep me safe
for I've been living in danger my whole life
and promise me that you'll finally give me
the home I've been trying to find
ever since the world kicked me out

BEGINNINGS & ENDINGS

I thought my love began with you
but now it seems like it will end with you too

PICK ONE

I'm not asking you to pick me
I'm asking you to pick *one*
because while you're deciding
you could lose us both

RUNNING

I like to run
I don't know if I am running away from something
or running toward something
I like to run
I don't know if I'm running to get lost
or running to be *found*

YOUR TEXT

Your text is two years late
but it's exactly what I need
and as if time hasn't changed a thing
and your texts still bring me back to life
and so do *you*

YOUR CALL

How can you tell I needed to hear from you
when I couldn't even whisper it to myself?
how come you still feel me
when I feel numb?

THE KEY TO MY HEART

I gave you a key to my heart
so you can be the only one to unlock it
but today I changed the lock
but I'd still like my old key back
because you don't deserve to have
access to any door of mine

UP CLOSE

Everything looks better from a distance
except for you
you look even better up close
you look even better with your flaws

YOUR MIRROR

I'm like your mirror
If you're beautiful
I will reflect your beauty
If you're ugly
I'll highlight your flaws
and if you break me
I will cut you

FATHER

I keep looking for you
in the arms of the wrong men
I try to find safety
in the middle of danger
I keep searching for a home
in the land of the homeless
but now I know
I can't look for you
when you're the one
I need to run away from

THE HOSPITAL

As I stayed waiting for the results
all I needed was your hand to hold
because there's nothing I couldn't handle
when you're standing right next to me
and even death won't scare me
when I know I'll die in your arms

IT'S NOT OVER YET

I only said goodbye
but I didn't say farewell
I only said I'm leaving
but I didn't say I'm giving up
I only said I can't take this anymore
but I didn't say I stopped loving you
I'm only giving you a pop quiz
not a final test

INDIFFERENT

Beneath your mask of ice
I see so much warmth
beneath your indifference
I see so much passion
beneath your cruelty
I see a man afraid of falling in love again

OLD SOUL

Maybe my soul is old
looking for a love that no longer exists
maybe my heart is old
born to endure so much pain

I FELL FOR YOU

I fell for you
like I've never fallen before
I don't blame myself for falling
I blame myself for thinking
you were strong enough
to catch me

ANOTHER DAY

Another day has passed and no one cared
another day has passed and I still can't love myself
another day has passed and I'm sad
another day has passed and I'm alone
another day has passed and I'm broken
another day has passed and I'm crying and no one
is listening
another day has passed and I failed myself
another day has passed and I'm celebrating someone
else's success
another day has passed and I still don't like who I see in
the mirror
another day has passed and I slept to my own lullaby
another day has passed and I left important words unsaid
another day has passed and you haven't found me yet
another day has passed and I'm glad it's over

CRITICS

Don't let their words grieve you
don't let their hatred tear you down
learn how to listen to them
and not hear them
learn how to look at them
and not see them

THE LAST NIGHT

Kiss me one last time

I'll love you tonight

because I'll forget you tomorrow

OPEN BOOK

I'm an open book

but you still can't read me

you can't sum me up in one headline

you can flip through my pages or highlight my words

but you will never be able to pin me down

because it takes more than reading from a distance
to know me

it takes more than a few words to figure me out

and it takes a lot more than reading to know my story

but you never had the courage to *finish* the story
'til the end

so you can read my book a thousand times

but you still won't be able to read *me*

PERFUME

You said you loved her perfume
and now you're trying to find it
in all cosmetics stores
not knowing that
it was the smell of the perfume
on *her* skin
that made it beautiful

THE WRONG GENERATION

Sometimes I feel like I don't belong to this generation
and sometimes I feel like
I actively participate in everything that's wrong with it

MOMENTS

They say life is nothing but
the moments that take our breath away
and I think they're right
but the problem is
these moments
were all with *you*

HOME

I come home and everything
feels the same
I come home and I feel
like nothing has changed
I come home and I remember
who I was
and then I remember
why I left

THE TRUTH

Tonight, I'll tell you how I feel
because I don't want to die tomorrow
and you still don't know that you're
the only one who kept me living
all those years

TO BE CONTINUED

Like an ending of a movie
we parted that night
but we both left with a smile
because we both knew
that this is not the end
this is only an *intermission*

DROWNING

In the depth of your eyes
I find myself drowning
and it's the kind of drowning
that I don't want to be saved from

I STILL WONDER ABOUT YOU

I wonder if you knew that I enjoyed every moment with you more than I enjoyed my entire life

I wonder if you think of me as someone who is so close yet so far away

I wonder if you are aware that so many words were left unsaid between us

and I wonder if you are curious to find out what they were

I wonder if I made it hard for you to sleep at night

I wonder if you worry that I might have met someone else

I wonder if you met someone else yourself

and I wonder if she will ever look at you the way I did

I wonder, even though there is no point in wondering

I wonder because deep down inside

I know you wonder too

YOUR LAUGH

I can still hear your laugh
echoing between those empty walls
but now you're laughing with her
and I can still hear your laugh
as I sit here and *weep*

THE ART OF LETTING GO

As you keep learning the art of letting go
let go of your fears, of your past,
of your mistakes, of your insecurities,
of your failures, of your self-doubt
forgive yourself enough to let go
of even the parts of you
that dim your light

LONELINESS

It's ironic that people underestimate loneliness and claim that they have no one by their side.

Loneliness is one big powerful person, loneliness is a ghost, loneliness is the elephant in the room, and loneliness is too much to handle sometimes.

If you look closely, *loneliness is you.*

BROKEN

Like a broken glass
you left me shattered
and now you want to
piece me back together
but how will you know who I am
when you no longer recognize who you see?
How will you know if I'm the same person
when every little piece of me
is not where it belongs?

FAMOUS

Sometimes I wish I was famous
and everyone knows my name
with all eyes on me
and sometimes I get scared
from the world
afraid of what people might see
when they scrutinize me

MY ESCAPE

I escape in my sleep
because my dreams have a place
in my sleep, I'm rich
in my sleep, I'm a role model
in my sleep, I'm beautiful
in my sleep, I'm *holding you*

ONE MOMENT

There a comes a moment in your life
when you feel that the whole world
conspired to disappoint you
and it hurts even more
when the world decides
not to be on your side

MY STORY

I want to write you in my book
but I'll be jealous
of all those other girls
who will fall in love with your *details*
when they read it

THE PERFECT MATCH

Every broken piece of you
seems to complete
every broken piece of me
and all the pieces of your broken heart
seem to make mine whole again

LIFE AS A HUMAN BEING

I'm learning to let things be
and I'm learning to look at life as a person
a person who is also still trying to figure it out
a person who is flawed
and a person who wants to be better on most days
but falls short on other days

PRISONER

I'm a prisoner of my own thoughts,
of all the feelings that torment me
I'm a prisoner in my own body
waiting for someone
to come set me free

YOU WILL ALWAYS BE MY DREAM

You will always be the dream that I'll never get
tired of asking for

the dream I want to dream every night

the dream I want to live every morning

and the dream that keeps me dreaming

LONG DISTANCE

But then I realized that distance was never the problem

it was always the person

the person who didn't want to commit to calling or visiting

the person who used distance as an excuse to get out of commitment altogether

but you give distance meaning

you give distance intimacy

because even though you're far away,

I can still feel you closer than anyone here

and I'd rather stay home talking to you on the phone

than spend the night in the arms of someone else

BLESSINGS

Days go by
and you understand why
some departures
were blessings in disguise

WITHOUT YOU

I realized that life is not about what you see
but more about who you see it with
I realized that the world is huge
but it still feels *empty*
without you in it

THIS IS WHY YOU SUDDENLY MISS ME

You miss me because you know
I will find someone better
You miss me because you know
you lost the best

LONGER NIGHTS

I wish the night was longer
so our conversations can never end
I wish the night could wait a little bit
until we're done talking about all the things
that kept us up at night all those years

WHAT WE HAD

Was it real?
Or was it all in my head?
Was it love?
Or was it *addiction?*

SORRY

I wish you could apologize
to something you broke
and it brings it back to what it was
without losing its core
I wish your 'sorry'
could undo the damage
that was scattered in the distance
you left between us
I wish your 'sorry'
could make me love you
while forgetting the pain
you've stricken me with

I WISH I WAS A TRAIN

I wish I was a train because trains don't wait for people
I wish I was a train because trains always know when to leave
trains always leave before it's too late
I wish I was a train because even when trains crash
they make the front page
even in their destruction
they still leave something for the world to talk about

SAVE THE LAST DANCE FOR ME

Ironically the lyrics of our song
talk about two people being together
after falling in love with other people
and as if we knew
that we had to find love away from each other
to realize that our love was special
to realize that our love was real
to know that I'm the one for you
and you're the one who's taking me home

ONE LAST TIME

I know we said goodbye before
but this is the last time
we're not going to say hello again
so hold me, *one last time*

THE ROAD

I don't know where the road may take us
but I'm enjoying the ride
because the bumps on the road don't matter
as long as you're the one driving

STORIES

Everyone has a story they can't tell

everyone has a story they'd like to forget

everyone has a story they read late at night when nobody is watching

because they still hope they can *rewrite* the ending

MESS

You didn't know that I'm messier than your mess
that your mess is order to me
you tried to mess me up
but you didn't know I thrive in *chaos*

TRAVELERS

And maybe we're all travelers
in search of significance
in search of solitude
in search of something inconceivable
in search of something fascinating
in search of our own treasure
in search of *ourselves*

LET ME GO

If I'm not the only one
let me go
If I'm not everything you need
let me go
If I don't make you smile from ear to ear
let me go
If you're not crazy about me
let me go

COLD

Their presence doesn't matter anymore
and their absence no longer hurts

YOU'RE GETTING MARRIED

You're getting married,
I always thought that on this day
it would be me standing right beside you
instead, I'm standing right behind her
waiting to catch the bouquet

I BLOCKED YOU TODAY

I blocked you today
because I was ready
to delete you
and your memories
from my life
I was ready to clean my news feed
getting rid of your dust

I'm over seeing what you like
and where you are
I'm over waiting for one like
or one comment from you
I'm done trying to impress you
when you're probably not even looking
I'm done fighting for your attention
when you're giving it to someone else

I blocked you today
because I wanted to remember who I was
before you came into my life
and made me hate myself
I blocked you because
I have to love myself
I blocked you so I could post things for me
instead of trying to send you a message.

Or maybe I'm trying to send
one final message to you:
you can't reach me anymore
you now belong to a list of strangers
I've never met
You now can't like my pictures
or see my posts
or see *me*

WINGS

You taught me how to fly

and then you tore my wings apart

WHEN BEAUTY TURNS UGLY

Sometimes in love, beauty is insecure
beautiful things would do anything to believe
that they are not beautiful
and sometimes beautiful things turn *ugly*

GOOD FRIENDS

If you have good friends, you will never feel unloved

If you have good friends, you will always have someone
to fix you when you're broken

If you have good friends, you will never be alone

If you have good friends, you have the world

FIREWORKS

We didn't just have a spark, we had fireworks

we wrote our names in the sand

and we told our secrets to the stars

and they swore they've never seen two people
shine so brightly together

we stole the show from the galaxies

we gave the world a love to remember

and together we wrote an unforgettable story

our love was *infinite*

we didn't just have a spark, we had fireworks

but fireworks are made to *explode*

PROBLEMATIC

The problem is...you're my problem
the problem is...I think I'm your problem too
the problem is...I'll never know

THE GIRL WHO LOVES TOO MUCH

And sometimes even her too muchness is not enough for her

she will always find ways to love you more

to hold you tighter

to pull you closer

to keep you safe

DON'T TELL THEM

Don't tell them why you're crying
because once they know the reason
behind your tears
they'll know how to make you cry

STUPID

It's stupid
to stay stuck on something
that ended years ago
but it's also stupid
to let it go
when it's everything
that you truly need

OMNIPOTENT

You're not in front of me
you're not even in the same city
so how could it be
that you're still all I see?

PARADISE

You held my hand
as we slow danced
under the moonlight
and for a moment
I felt like I was in paradise
and your arms took me to heaven

THIS IS HOW YOU KNOW

If you miss me, you should call me
If you care, you need to show me
If you want me, you have to fight for me
and if you love me, you must tell me

SERENDIPITY

I met you when I wasn't looking
I bumped into you when I was looking for someone else
but I found you
and you turned out to be
better than anyone I was looking for

EVERYTHING

I'll never be the girl who feels nothing
I'll always be the girl who feels *everything*

SAME OLD

I say you're a changed man now
and I open my heart to you once more
then you break it again
and I'm reminded
that some people
never really change

TOO LATE

You're not allowed to come back
after you've left
you're not allowed to hold me
after you've let me go

THIS IS WHAT YOU TAUGHT ME

You taught me that I can't depend on you
you taught me that you'll never be there
you taught me not to call you when I need you
and you taught me how to take care of myself
because you couldn't take care of me

YOU WANT ME, I WANT HIM

I don't know if I want you
or I'm only pretending that I do
because the one that I really want
doesn't really want me

THE SEA

The sea makes me long for the past
when the sea was my playground
instead of being an ocean
that drains my sorrow

YOUR NAME

Your name makes me think of you as an experience
a memory
a lesson
a painting that was supposed to be beautiful
but turned out all *squiggly*

HARD TO LOVE

They tell me I'm hard to love
and I secretly feel it deep inside
but you're the only one
who made it look so easy
you're the only one who loved me
without complaining
and maybe this is why
I can *hardly* love anyone
after you

POLAR OPPOSITES

I left you in peace
and you left me in pieces

DARLING, IT'S MORE THAN JUST A DANCE

It's just a dance they say
but sometimes it's all you need
let the music sway you left and right
in the arms of the one you love
living in the music
living in the moment
moving our bodies
and moving our souls

YOU

Everyone has that person they can't forget
everyone has that person they'll always take back
everyone has that person they'll always miss
everyone has that person they wish they could start over with
everyone has that person they'll never stop loving
and I have all that
I have all that with *you*

WHAT IS LOVE

I know I have options
but I'm scared of relationships
but you make me fearless
you make me forget that I was ever hurt
you make me walk through the walls I've built
and if this is not love
I don't know what is

ON YOUR WEDDING DAY

If you ever feel like you're not good enough for him
I want you to remember today
and the way he looked at you
as you were walking down the aisle
I want you to remember that he chose you
to be his *forever*

A STRONG WOMAN'S PRIDE

This is why she didn't say hello
this is why she didn't respond to your text
this is why she didn't wish you a happy birthday
this is why she stayed away all these years
this is why she's *cold*
this is why she will never say she misses you
and this is why she will never say she still loves you

AIRPORTS

Everyone has someone waiting for them
some holding flowers
some holding gifts
others giving hugs
most giving kisses
and here I am
arriving and returning
and no one is waiting for me
wondering when the day will come
when airports won't make me *cry*

SEASONS OF YOU

I think of you in summer
when the sun is shining
and I long for your light
but I crave you in winter
when everyone is so cold
and I long for your warmth

YOU WILL NEVER KNOW ME

You will never know me
if you're always looking around
and I'll never show you
who I really am
if you don't try to *see* me

SUNSETS AND SUNRISES

And in the most romantic city in the world
I didn't miss you
because if you were the one
I wouldn't be here alone
and you wouldn't have left

TIMELESS

Your love is timeless
others come and go
but you remain the same
others try to fight
but you always win
others try to sweep me off my feet
and I find my legs
running back to you

YOU CAME BACK

The universe brought you back to me
in an unexpected night
and it was exactly what I needed
to finally understand
why you had to leave
and why you can't come back again

BACKBONE

You told me you'll have my back
but you broke it
when you couldn't lift
both me and my baggage
so you *dropped* us both

HER NAME

And it's in the way you said her name
that I knew she's more than just a friend
and it's in the way you said mine
that I knew that I'm no longer the one you need

PATIENCE

She could be the most patient person in the world
when she is waiting for you
but she could also be the cruelest person you've ever met
when she decides that she's done *waiting*

ETERNAL

You'll never die
because you've lived inside my heart once
and my heart
is *eternal*

THE FINAL PLAY

Life is nothing but a play
you either act well
and let people applaud you
or grab a seat
and applaud all those
who played you

MOTHER

I roamed the world
looking for happiness and heaven
only to find them
in your loving arms

SEPARATED

We both went our separate ways
but something whispers to me that
we still belong together
that our paths will cross again
and never part ways
that our separation
was only a *bridge*
to connect us back
when we're both done
rebuilding ourselves

I'M THE ONE FOR YOU

Even when you're far away
we both know
that I'm closer to you
than any other woman
and no matter how many women
you take to your bed
I'm the one you'll always think of
before you go to sleep

LET ME TALK ABOUT YOU

You love how my eyes sparkle
when I talk about what I'm passionate about
so please let me
talk more about *you*

YOUR EYES

Your eyes are beautiful
I get lost in them
I just wish
they only looked at me

YOUR WISH

Be patient
maybe God is planning to
grant it to you
the way you asked for it
but at *his* convenience

THIS ONE IS FOR YOU

As the sun sets in Santorini
and the stillness sets in my head
I wonder how different my life would be
if I had ever told you
all the words I should have said.

ABOUT THE WRITER

Rania Naim grew up in Cairo, Egypt with more than just a passion for writing, it was her dream. Rania's passion for writing bloomed when she realized that she wants to dedicate her time bringing personal stories to life. Her stories are all inspired by true events and by everyday conversations. As a writer for Thought Catalog, Rania writes about life, love, work and the pursuit of your best tomorrow. Rania now lives in Washington, DC learning more about people, life, love and the world. For more information about Rania, visit:

Twitter—twitter.com/Ranianaim

Instagram—instagram.com/ranianaim

Facebook—facebook.com/Ranianaimpage

Website—ranianaim.com

Other THOUGHT CATALOG titles
published by AMARYLLIS in India

THE PIVOT YEAR

THE MOUNTAIN IS YOU

WHEN YOU'RE READY THIS IS HOW YOU HEAL

101 ESSAYS THAT WILL CHANGE THE WAY YOU THINK

CEREMONY

THIS WAS MEANT TO FIND YOU:
WHEN YOU NEEDED IT MOST

THIS IS ME LETTING YOU GO

SALT WATER

EVERYTHING YOU'LL EVER NEED
YOU CAN FIND WITHIN YOURSELF

THE HUMAN ELEMENT

THE STRENGTH IN OUR SCARS

THE TRUTH ABOUT EVERYTHING